"Susan Frybort is that rarest of poets, a true visionary whose every line is forged out of inmost experience and whose language is sensuous, direct and embodied. Very few modern poets risk entering the territory she has embraced so bravely and with such dogged and precise passion. She subtitles this book, *Poems to Encourage*. Read these poems and let them arouse in you the courage you most need in our devastating times—the courage to experience and embody your own divine reality and put it into action on every level of your renewed life."

—ANDREW HARVEY, author of *Turn Me to Gold: 108 Translations of Kabir* and *The Hope*

"*Look to the Clearing* offers rare and intimate companionship to anyone alert to the yearnings of their personal journey. With compassion for all that the soul's path might bring to your doorstep, this volume offers insight and inquiry in equal measure, understanding that the spark of a question can ignite the truest quest of your heart. Frybort is not just alive to the paradoxes of our humanness—she helps us find guidance, clarity and even comfort within their midst."

—PHILIP SHEPHERD, author of *Radical Wholeness*, *Deep Fitness* and *New Self, New World*

"Susan Frybort's poems are so much more than just poems: they are invocations with the power of a centuries-old prayer; they are insights into how the culture you're embedded in has skewed your perceptions; they are beautiful yet fierce

reminders of our uniqueness; and they are, above all, portals through which the world can be brought more vividly into focus. Some you might want to memorize—that their wisdom might be close enough to hold you in difficult times. Others will inspire you to fall in love with the beauty of your being and all that we live amongst. Open these pages and tumble into the delight and wonder that they so clearly illuminate."
—ALLYSON WOODROOFFE, embodiment coach and co-director of The Embodied Present Process

"In *Look to the Clearing*, Susan Frybort's poetry expresses the deepest emotions of life in ways that honor the human spirit while acknowledging both the triumphs and the struggles. Susan's poetry is a celebration for everyone who suffered as a child and through healing now "brings pure light into this world." There is a poem for every phase of healing and profound encouragement for stepping bravely into life. This book of poetry is a must read for all who are on the healing path!"
—JANYNE MCCONNAUGHEY, Ph.D., author of *Brave: A Personal Story of Healing Childhood Trauma*

"Susan Frybort's *Look to the Clearing* is an inspiring collection of transformational poems. Highly recommended for anyone who is ready to acknowledge and heal their trauma!"
—THEO FLEURY, NHL Stanley Cup Champion, leading voice in relational trauma

"Susan has given us another great masterpiece about the heart and its challenging and valuable journey through life. Her new book is indeed a painting that will continuously delight us and nurture our soul. What I always love about

Susan's work is that it is so firmly grounded in the truth of our human authenticity, as well as so rich in delightful images and metaphors. No false promises and no apologies for our humanity, rather an honoring of the human spirit with its tears and its laughter, its mishaps and breakthroughs, its trembling as well as its amazing courage. This precious book honors the fragility and the grief of our self as well as the splendor of love. This precious book calls on us to deeply value, appreciate and love the full authenticity of who we are and what we go through. I highly and insistently recommend it for everyone and every household, to be enjoyed, shared and also passed to our young ones who so much need to hear its message! A book filled with warmth and real uncommon wisdom—to be read again and again!"

—CHRIS SAADE, life coach and author of *Rebellion of the Heart: Deep Authenticity, Bold Love, Passion, Strength, & Global Solidarity*

"Susan's poetry is vulnerable, powerful, deep and eloquent. Her words transcend the mind and speak directly to the heart. This book heals the parts of us that are left behind in conventional healing models. Highly recommended!"

—DR. MITCH ABRAMS, founder of NexGenHealth

"In this third volume of her poetry, Susan Frybort continues to midwife the awakening process, offering hope and reassurance to readers in navigating the awakening, healing and growing process, especially in the troubling, unsettled times in which we now find ourselves. In language that is earthy and organic, the author draws from the natural world—the world of dandelions, songbirds, lavender, thyme, storms and seasons—

evoking images that appeal to the senses juxtaposed against a bold, unflinching exploration into the demons that haunt us: fear, regret, failure, and uncertainty. Though confronting and probing, her words are gentle, nurturing and intimate, often addressing the reader directly and ever-so-knowingly, as "you," enfolding readers into the commonality of our shared, lived experience and affirming the surety that within ourselves—within our bodies, our souls and each other—we have the resources we need to heal, to awaken, and ultimately to discover and embrace our callings."

—BARBARA BORUFF, author and poet,
Master of Theological Studies

LOOK TO THE
CLEARING

POEMS TO ENCOURAGE

SUSAN FRYBORT

ENREALMENT PRESS
TORONTO, CANADA

Published by Enrealment Press
PO Box 65618,
Dundas, Ontario,
Canada L9H-6Y6

Cover photo by © Nataba| istockphoto.com
Cover Background by jessicahyde | istockphoto.com
Author photos by Lindsay Knapp
Cover design by Susan Frybort
Book design by Allyson Woodrooffe

Printed in the USA

Library and Archives Canada Cataloguing in Publication

Title: Look to the clearing : poems to encourage / Susan Frybort.
Names: Frybort, Susan, 1966- author.
Identifiers: Canadiana (print) 20210285486 | Canadiana (ebook) 20210285494 | ISBN 9781988648071
   (softcover) | ISBN 9781988648088 (HTML)
Subjects: LCGFT: Poetry.
Classification: LCC PS3606.R93 L66 2021 | DDC 811/.6—dc23

In loving memory of
Heidi Annaliese Boruff

LOOK TO THE CLEARING

POEMS TO ENCOURAGE

SUSAN FRYBORT

EVEN THE HEALER NEEDS

Sometimes we are exactly what we need.

Eventually, the helper will need assistance.
The encourager will need uplifting.
The comforter needs reassurance,
and even the healer needs to be healed.

Through our emotional needs, life makes itself known,
exposes our similarities and insists on the importance
of connection within the warmth of empathetic presence.

Developing an awareness of what we need to be healthy,
to take in love and to feel safe in the world, then cultivating
clear and peaceful language to express each one vulnerably,
is a process that can open the door to harmony.

So, may you learn to listen and follow your heart's
insistent cries of longing—back to the origin of
your earliest pains and bring forward your needs
to be heard, finally, with recognition,
understanding and acceptance.

And may you likewise know the content and deserving
blessing of feeling met and tenderly received.

YOU WERE THE LIGHT ALL ALONG

You were the light all along.
You needn't wait anymore
on the arrival of grand champions
or spiritual giants
when you are the final hero
of your life story.
It was you who struggled with God
and wrestled with demons
in the face of everyday conflict.
It was you who unsheathed
a blade of determination
to slash through the brush of daily fear.
It was you who sank into
the very depths of yourself, then
trudged through the sludge of pain
to find the hidden parts
silently praying for healing.

It is you, bright child.

And it is the stuff born out
of your darkest of days
that brings pure light
into this world.

MISSION

To survive you had to pay attention. You had to listen and learn the rules, then follow them closely. But your needs were kept from being expressed inside these rules. Eventually, you began to question the validity of your needs, and even lost trust in your own judgement.

When you must hide what you really want or require, there is no space for confidence to fly freely. There's no room for trust to grow. No opportunity to learn from what it is you've been craving. It's not joyous or satisfying when you make it your main purpose to please others and reject your hunger to actualize.

Now your walk, your steadfast mission, becomes about *you*. Your survival defenses are no longer required and your responses to appease are ready to be released. And your new practice is to allow yourself to express and unquestionably believe in your deepest needs.

SOULMATE

Soulmate of mine,
you are not passing through,
not slipping away in the night,
but taking the journey with me.
We'll bring along our best tools
to capture a passionate life
and slay the dark giants together.
We'll wrestle issues to the ground
to understand or get it right,
burning the midnight oil
if we need to.
Let's learn what it means
to accept the conditions,
appreciate the limitations,
and delve into our own separate caverns.
Because when I throw myself
at the mercy of your love,
I am healed in ways
I could never imagine.

OPENINGS

You're not slipping through the cracks, but *falling into openings*. That certain person. A remarkable thing. The sudden event. A season of hardship. Being diagnosed. Falling in and out of love. An intense phase of feeling lost. Or the death that stopped the clocks and shook your world...

Something dropped you to your knees, only to pick you up again, and thrust you into an unexpected entrance of a life-changing opening.

An opening where everyday existence and the core of your being collapse into one, and nothing feels the same again. You are not being neglected, not being ignored. Instead, a great spirit speaks to you. A conversation between this source and your soul is significant and ongoing—and it had always been. But you can hear it much clearer since passing through the opening.

Listen as it reveals:
The strength of your connection is just as powerful as the sun.
You are awesomely comprised of wisdom and creation.
You are not all alone, but guided by intuition.
And while here on earth, you are a complete universe holding a continuance of profound experiences with spiritual meaning.

WILD HORSE

You marched to the beat of a colorful drum.
You swam against the traditional tide.
You did what was not expected,
living your life outside the box
of imposed ideas.
Yet, they didn't see you coming,
break through the gate or rush the stands;
pushing past the standard pack
with your visions, goals and plans.
And when they were running elsewhere,
you took the usual by storm.
So cheers to you, the great wild horse,
who refused to settle down
to become trained or be contained,
while the others ran behind you
in circles that conformed.

WHY ARE YOU BEING SO BUSY?

The message was to keep busy. So we kept busy. Sometimes out of shame, sometimes to avoid certain truths. Most times to survive. To be made to feel lazy and useless if you didn't stay busy is what we experienced on a collective level, perhaps so we wouldn't slow down and thaw. Maybe to prevent us from asking the important questions. What frequency do you want to live on? How do you want to design your life around time? How is a powerful system capitalizing on my energy? What was so traumatic for me that the one thing I want to do is not stop and think about it and feel into its pain, or protect myself from reliving a sense of lack? Why do I think if I look busy, I am enough? What does productivity mean to you if the fruit is never within your reach?

YOU ARE NOT THE WRECKAGE

It's when you figured out how doing the things you love makes you feel alive, the joy rippling from the breadth of your being becomes the sweetest revenge. It's when you align with peace by accepting how the violations against your body and spirit were never meant as a gift from God. It's when you take in how it's not a need for a cure, but sometimes it's a natural need for comfort and assurance to allay the pain.

You know now, you don't have to keep moving and altering, shifting or hiding. You understand healing isn't an activity or an expectation required to be whole, and it's not always something you want to share in an upload or therapy session.

It looks like tender skin gradually forming over what was once a searing burn when you slow down, when you rest, or when you're patient and try something new. It looks like validating moments when you ache and days when you can't stop crying. It's when the memory doesn't go away but the exhale from remembering releases a little easier than it used to. It even looks like letting some things inside of you be what they are and loving them in the condition they're in.

It's when you turn on the light and look around to see, yes, there was damage done, but you are not the wreckage.

ILLUSTRIOUS BEINGS

It was in my weakest moments
that I discovered inner-strength.

It was after my sincere and heartfelt
confessions, I heard untold wisdom.

It was when I professed my limitations,
I recognized the infinite depth within.

Throughout life and by
love's unseen hands,

I am formed and informed and reformed
with each new understanding.

We are illustrious beings,
shaped by what we have survived.
Healed by our own hearts.
Crafted with care.
Always in the making.

SILENT VAPORS

Everything you thought you had; everything you believed it was; everything they appeared to be, seemed to transform unexpectedly into a silent vapor memory. And all that loss found its way into your chest and throbbed against the pulse of living.

You learned mourning does not rely upon an efficient and selective process. It took a season—and another season, and another—to walk through each tract of land set before you. You learned grief itself is an unmapped journey you would inevitably experience, and might become lost among the non-sequential complex layers. You learned we all carry the death of someone, something, or someplace around inside, and for that, we need not ever feel ashamed. A marriage, a sibling, a child, a friendship, a calling. A mission, a beloved companion, a way of being.

Try to stifle the soul's crying. Try to bundle up and hide the monumental *Whys*, only to learn that to surrender and fully plumb the depths of sorrow can grief be free to move and breathe through the runnels of your heart.

Even while you own the newest moments—even as you go through the motions of an active and unfolding life.

LAVENDER AND THYME

Life, in its tonal range, holds impatience and grace every day,
and every day is intent on slipping by with fine-spun
meaning.

Only when she's growing old, do you finally realize you never
deeply knew her. Only when an illness weakens, can you feel
the close and gentle nature of real care. Only when the rain
forces you inside, can you appreciate the aromas dancing with
pleasure.

It seems like only when you're still and silent, you can hear
the conversation between resilient roots and fleeting leaves.

They tell of how it is the tender things can break and mend
a heart. Of how it is while two slowly drift apart,
somewhere else another two will stay together.

And we,
we talk about the vulnerability in honesty;
about our long-held fears and the irony
of how convenience sometimes made ignoring easy.

We say,
it seems like only when we're pressed,
like lavender and thyme,
is when life invariably leaves behind
an intense, yet soft and earthy scent we find
we'll always remember.

BLESS ALL BRAVE THINGS

The prayer I cannot pray.
The words that rest unspoken.
The feelings that can't be named.
The grief that bursts wide open.

The cry that turned to laughter.
The smile that broke the ice.
The pain that was cut off.
The poem I couldn't write.

Life, bless all the forming things
that escape or remain in me;
those resisting to be seen,
and the ones that risk
coming out
as brave beginnings.

THE POWER OF MY WHOLENESS

With time I understood a self-deepening truth.
My wounds, my setbacks,
my flaws, and my mistakes
are to be met with my entire heart.
My feelings of overwhelm.
My moments of bewilderment.
My perceived weaknesses
and my unresolved trauma.
Every vulnerable piece of me
calls out to be seen as an opening to acceptance.
A portal to forgiveness. And even more,
an entryway to seeing, feeling, and believing
in the power of my wholeness.

LET YOUR LOVE FLOW

Let your love flow. Step closer to your humanness and embrace the imperfections of your lived experiences, involvements and relationships as discoveries blazing new tracks inside previously unknown territory that lead you into fuller connections.

Let your love go. Let it meet you in the setbacks and deep-rooted regrets wafting through, questioning whether or not you did enough of the right things to secure a forming bond. Caress your grieving heart and soothe past yearnings to be held in a certain style and warmth by others who are, in their way, deeply searching for themselves, yet not entirely ready to unfurl and be seen.

Let your love show up for you. Especially when you feel yourself shutting down because you fear you gave away too much. Let your love go into the places unvoiced within. The places where your desires and wounding around intimacy have their own longings to reveal just how worthy and endearing you really are in this world.

Let your love flow...

EAGLE
(MOVING ON)

Because you can no longer ignore you've been holding it in,
as if it could transform you or become transformed,
while it tirelessly asks, *why do you stay?*

Because you are no longer willing to be just where you are,
folding yourself into the scene, reluctant to leave while feeling
boxed in—gratefully seeing, yet no longer being
anything less or anything more.

Because under the skin of that ennui, this acceptance,
and those traces of weariness aches a sliver, tacitly piercing
the tenderest sides of your soul.

And it will persistently do so,
until the point when you decide to pull it out, set it down,
cross the room and walk out the door.

The eagle perched above her empty nest can go now.

Because settling in and listening to what remains
of her fading sorrow is becoming less important
than surfacing elsewhere, breathing in new air
of a nurturing current
as she regally soars.

Look up and hear these words I say, you will be alright in
the core of your soul. If you are heartbroken by separation,
you will feel a gentle breeze slip past the curtains and brush
against your grief. If you are tired from a strident world,
you will find assurance in the stillness of night. If you are
frightened by what is unknown, you will take slow breaths
and calm the pace of your mind. When there's no one beside
you to lend needed support, you will feel held by something
not grand and sudden, and not by a manifestation appearing
like magic and light. Instead, you will sense an immense
peace filling the room you inhabit, as it soothes today's panic
and worry away.

MARK THIS SPOT

Whatever happens, however it turns out, celebrate your endurance. Honor what it took to get through. Don't guilt out over checking out when you needed. There's nothing wrong with hiding when you've had enough and for coming out to honestly speak what's been on your mind or share what's in your heart. It wasn't a disgrace to sift out what felt harmful. Remember your connection to something loving, something merciful, something peaceful, yet strong. Whichever way it turns out to be, *mark this spot* as your moment of truth.

STAY IN YOUR LIGHT TODAY

Stay in the light
today—
just stay.

Don't be swept
off course by a rush
of mishandling waves.
Stay in your light
today—
stay.

Empowerment is intrinsically yours and is not bestowed
as a gift or worn as an archetype, but is created by you and
established within as your lighthouse. Built brick by brick on
internal ground from everything you've worked through and
continually process. All the courageous, sovereign, intuitive,
and wise parts of you come together to embolden your truth.

Thus, in life the dark clouds will rise,
the sudden gales will crash and throw,
and your soul set adrift on stormy seas.
Look inward as the guide to come back to yourself.

Stay in your light
and stand tall.

GRATITUDE KNOWS

Gratitude will not casually dismiss all your heartache, your suffering, your fear, and disease—or make them vanish into the morning air. But she does have caring arms enough to evenly hold you.

Gratitude knows, to view life through a lens of thankfulness is no mere task in a world where there are still many unanswered needs, and while it feels unjust to reflect, *had it not been for God's grace, I have escaped the misfortune another must duly endure.* Or when there is pain in your body, or a loss you're trying to make sense of, or a challenge you can't overcome.

Gratitude understands the human condition, and with a whisper invites you to recognize the earth's honest blessings. To let your appreciation for life rise like gentle breaths into a flowing stream. To give thanks for what is good. To see the gifts you hadn't seen before. To let it prompt you to open the door and make room for another. To spread your table with sustenance and invite the lonely in from isolating winds.

In return, gratitude will strengthen your weariness and soothe lavender salve upon your troubled mind. She will soften your countenance and deepen your connections. She will lift you from restriction and into love's expanding grace. And your broken heart will fare better than before, in the shelter of her calm, protective arms.

LIFELINE

Today you may be feeling like the most misunderstood
person in the world, drowning in feelings of guilt,
inadequacy, anxiety or overwhelm—
all threatening to push you too far.

The good news is, on a day like today,
love throws out a lifeline.

You may need to lift your head
a bit higher just to see it,
or extend your heart a little
further to reach for it.
You might have to row
a short way past the fog
to believe it.

Even so, love is here for you
in the sweetness of each opening morning.
In the smile of that one passerby.
In the very preciousness of the air you are breathing.

Yes, love is here and now and always
offering its saving grace to embrace you.

Today. Right where you are.

REFLECTIONS

Sometimes you can get in the
way of feeling the waters of joy.

Sometimes it's not actually you being a
stumbling block, but a genuine challenge.

Sometimes the reflection you see
tells more than you're saying.

Sometimes the discomfort and anguish are symptoms
of not making room for all you're becoming.

And sometimes, you have to decide you're tired
of carrying this bucket of sadness and risk moving on.

ON THE OUTSKIRTS OF DISAPPOINTMENT

To the *What Might Have Beens*,
washing in and draining out,
reminding me of *What Will Never Be*,
like vibrant colors too hard to forget
or scented longings from another world.

To the sweet visions of possibility
dissolving before my very eyes.
To situations reversing position,
quite sly and suddenly.

As I let the layers of each let-down
be sloughed and peel away,
a brighter view is on my side
and is revealed.

I found on the outskirts of disappointment
waits the heart of gratitude,
sincerely holding my appreciation
for *What Is* and *Right Now*.

YOU CAN SPEAK NOW, CHILD

The blisters from abuse had been sheathed in
an impenetrable silence for too long.
Because what proved just as traumatic as a child's burden
of not ever telling, was to be left feeling powerless
living among the flames of shame and confusion.

O child, you don't have to press the guilt
of another's wrongdoing into your soul
to carry as your own any longer.
No matter how old you've grown,
no matter how remote, you are never too far
from being held safe by your revealing.

You can speak now child,
your words were never lost in the fire,
nor your essence any lessened.

From out of you grows a fertile shoot that is the entire forest.
Out of you a faint bird becomes the mighty flock itself.
Out of the ashes of your innocence,
an entire kingdom has risen.

THE UNVEILING

Everything yet incomplete offers a perspective. A perspective on how it was never all about the end result. It was never about the impressive tree, the fresh skin of a former wound, or crossing the finish line. It wasn't even exactly about the seed of the tree itself.

It's about the energy; the nurturing, the loving and the cultivating. It's about the separating and severing before the actual planting. It's about the holding back and cutting off, the releasing of mourning. It's about the reaching out as well as the sequestering. It's about allowing for unfolding and developing, and making way for a process to occur.

It's about exploring the recesses of anger and reaching deep, deep down and really feeling the sadness. And it's even about expressing possibilities. It's about giving and being receptive. It is about all things opening a way for healing and wholeness to be seen. It's about realizing that you are complete, and the work is allowing your wholeness to come into view.

It is about the entire experience.

So, may you meld readily into becoming, less concerned about what isn't finished, and more on living heart-centered—tending to that which unveils the essence of *you*.

IT'S TIME TO BE FREE

It's time to be free of all your useless worry.

The worry you've repeated in your mind
so often, it's become a brooding mantra—
the distress that tosses and turns at
night and steals your peaceful sleep.

It's time to knock away the fret that's hardened
into an anchor on your shoulders;
it's time to dismiss each *What Could Happen*
and say goodbye to *What Might Be.*

You're not destined to become a flightless
bird on this amazing journey,
but called to rest your mind in grace
and let your spirit soar with ease.
It's time to fly from inner phantoms
that hold no power of completion.

Dear heart, it's time to gather up
your needless worry and release.

THE FIRES OF SWEET RELEASE

You can take all the time you need before you approach the
fires of sweet release, when you have spent a life wrestling
the pain suppressed in distant memories. Addiction. Self-
harm. Substance abuse. Self-doubt. *Prepare yourself.* It is no
small task to go inside your nearest impressions, then deep
into the bedrock of what you've come up against to collect
what's been held onto for so long that they've become
ingrained as fixed beliefs.

What comes up wants to be seen.
Like your fear of being left all alone.
Your experiences with isolation.
The loss of parental guidance.
The lack of love and tenderness.
The anger from feeling betrayed,
and all that remains from the excessive
acquisition of emotional heartache.

You have survived so much. There is a fire that burns
for ancestral wounds. Now gather the sticks of invisible
hoardings into a bundle to be named and believed. It's no
small achievement, when you have overcome great odds, to
trust you'll find the courage held inside to emblazon an alter
of ceremonial fire.

And thereafter, may you be washed in newborn ease.
May your spirit dance and your laughter finally play beyond
the house that held the pain of old, neglected wounds.

THE BLESSING IN EACH PROGRESSION

Just when I feel
the settling in
of a calm routine,
life has a way
of flipping the script.
Change has a way
of bursting in
to reshuffle the scene.

As I mature
and set my ways,
may I learn to cope
with transformation,
bittersweet.

And when I say
farewell
to former things
that held the space,
may I see the blessing
in each progression
that arrives
to take their
place.

CALLINGS

What you have done with your life is inspiring,
not because you packaged it to present,
not because you met each day to be productive,
not because you made a big contribution,
not because you became a brand.
But because as you attune to yourself—
and by looking inside you've discovered the gifts
unique to your aliveness. The gifts that reveal
a specific purpose and personal meaning.

You've answered your calling.

Born on earth, wrapped in flesh we come,
each one not fully knowing how to live
or understanding how to die.
But in between, we instinctively feel
our pact with life is to bundle up all
the explanations we possibly can
and discover what it is we have inside to give.

You've answered your calling.

HERE'S TO CONFUSION

Here's to confusion.
Here's to patterns being disrupted by life's
unpredictable tempo. Here's to not knowing,
yet somehow grasping I can withstand and bend
just like open waters; being receptive to the teachings
of contrast and change and to finally seeing.

Here's to lost footing. Here's to being thrown off balance
and breaking through my deep-grooved thinking
and outdated styles of perceiving.
Here's to walking into waves of fresh ideas
and colliding with radical ways of being.

Here's to frustration and disorientation.
Here's to climbing out of the rut of habits
and swimming into sweet waters of freedom.
Here's to discomfort and dissatisfaction;
how they lead me to deeper paths
and redirect my attention to
the light of alternative reason.

Here's to pains of truth overcoming erroneous roots.
When even the simple things become strangely complicated,
here's to forming new concepts, gathering bold insights,
and to gaining with each untried day,
a life deeply lived, spilling over with meaning.

YOUR PERSONAL HEALING

Your personal healing has never been done before.
Not by anyone but you.
So be patient, gentle, merciful and kind
as you attempt to uncover, untangle, revisit
and reclaim while you're inside the vast field
of emotions within the process of working through.

This means you'll be required to reshuffle and sort
an array of misplaced feelings. Don't sprint through
the tall grass, past the wildflowers of misinterpretations
enroute to recapturing and restoring what has been lost
or became disrupted, rather own the turf you're standing on.

And all you held that was never really yours—
like the guilt for not doing enough, any blame
for upsetting the current, all the pushback
for taking your rightful space—let it fall to the ground.

Then from here on out, despite the ups and downs, remember:
You don't have to pick up everything that gets thrown at you.

ONE PRAYER

Let me be soft in times when it's essential.
Help me to be sensitive enough to feel
wet drops quench my skin
when there come gentle rains,
and the feathery sweep of air
caress my face
like the tender brush
of a dove's wing.

And let me hear
the clear and quiet manner
of another soul
whispering into mine.

Let me shed again and again
what never matters in the end,
until my core has ample space
to grow resilient and strong.

That I might learn by heart
how setting down
what no longer serves my body,
my breath, and my mind,
becomes my most meaningful
and truest of offerings.

GRIEF WHISPERS

Even after you tell it all the gentle things
you know how to say, and even after
you've cried your last lingering goodbye,

there's a certain pain that swells up
while you're not looking—
jumps out the box to swallow you whole,
before grief whispers yet a deeper wisdom.

It says,

that thing you wanted,
that person you loved,
that moment passed,
held so much meaning
and came with you
all the way
to where you stand
right now.

One day, the pain
needn't remind you so much
as will the purest moment
of simply knowing.

OUT OF THE ORDINARY

It's a remarkable thing coming out of the ordinary; the place where living lessons can be found in life's quiet, commonplace moments and phases. A place where good and bad things happen to everyone and people grow through personal challenges, seeing one another in the reflections of their struggle. The place where dreams may be buried under a pile of responsibilities, but where redemption flows in the wake of mistakes and lost chances. The place where you live close to the ground and even if creation sometimes has to wait in line, there's no expiration date on imagination.

And while you're in there—convinced that you're existing off the radar in some meaningless swirl of activities, making peanut butter sandwiches and sorting laundry—you never fully realize how heroic it is to raise a child and manage the workings of the ordinary life. You never think of this time as the best sort of wine, growing intensely sweet with every year in passing.

You never imagine how these established rituals will one day wrap your soul in the rarest form of comfort.

What if you found out, just in time,
your most genuine and meaningful of offerings
is to set down what no longer serves
your body, breath, and peace of mind?

A CALLING

A calling
isn't concerned
about fame,
or interested
in glory.
Callings
are not providers
of comfort
and sometimes lead
to sacrifice.
And not everyone
will answer
the loud cries
coming from something
voracious
deep inside that's
wanting to wake them
into living full-on with
purposeful passion.

THE EXISTENTIAL QUEST

You can spend the waking hours analyzing every angle of
what went wrong, piecing together each *would*, *could*, and
should in the hope it will cover the situation with value and
meaning, yet miss the point of appreciation altogether. And
you can find several decent answers that will boil down
just fine and bring you to the bottom line. You can go all
over the map, if you want to. You can even live with the
outstanding question. But if nothing makes sense when you
desire it most, and if you find your toes pointing towards not
even close, you can remember this:

The revelation at the end of the existential quest is that life
is to be embraced—furthermore, enjoyed rather than be
perfectly understood, and that you take the ordinary stuff
living inside it and uplift it into art and beauty and song,

and that you relate and connect and thread your life into the
heart of humanity.

Last of all, in the time you are here, love fiercely another
soul and make peace with your own.

JUST BEING

Sometimes *just being* needs space to relax. It needs time to pause from the pressure of living up to the duties and expectations of a rigid framework, or rest from showing up in full armour everyday to protect a tender internal truth. Or sometimes *just being* needs to cry and feel into coarse emotions for awhile. Whatever it takes for all the layers of what has built up inside begin to unwrap the gift you truly are, deep within, *just being*.

WHAT WE LEAVE

It's not on the globe
or a map,
what remains
when we leave.

It's the prayers,
and the songs,
and the love,
and the seeds.

It's the echo of words spoken
all our pain and grief,
and each penetrating regret
we no longer need.

I pick up the banner of light within.
Torn and mended again and again.
I pick up the banner and raise it high—
everything I thought would break me
taught me more of who I am.

WRINKLED LINES

You can read so much in a face
worn with love and etched by time,
where each crease joins another, scrawling out
the unspoken words of a passionate story
—where lay written
every moment of sadness and worry,
baring the places where burdens were buried,
and where joy broke the tensions
and elations remain, annunciated
in the flecks of bright eyes.

Wrinkled lines are
a biographical account
of a life lived earnestly.
A life lived with imperfections.
A life inhabited with meaning.

I SAID GOODBYE TO OLD KEYS

I said goodbye to old keys,
faded welcome mats, too;
chipped porcelain, torn feelings,
and fragmented dreams.

I said goodbye to past things
that were no longer true:
Bad connections, warped reflections,
and high expectations I couldn't hold to.

I said goodbye to old pain,
bitter tears and dull varnish;
so long wishes that waned,
or got covered with tarnish.

I said goodbye to old keys
that open doors obsolete—
'bye to staying too long
when it's better to leave.

And goodbye to the land of fabricated ideals;
goodbye make believe. Hello what is real.
Goodbye over-thinking, hello let it be.
I said, hello cloudless mind,
rolling hills and new scenes.

THE CALL OF LOVE

You keep pursuing something greater within yourself, and you do it through the call of love. You keep longing to dive further into something else, and that something wanting to be met is your truth. Sometimes you go in, then pull back, wait it out and go in again, only to dance your way around it. One more time, you show up and lean in closer to be heard.

There you stand, exposed and vulnerable all over again. You get scared. It might get shaky. You might fall down and even lose yourself, or mess it up well beyond its former recognition. But for every time you fell down, for every night you lost your way, for every lie you told, and every time you turned up underprepared and unrehearsed, there it is still waiting for you, undisturbed.

Your truth is a song only you can sing.

And when a certain thing, that destined person, or repeating lesson comes back around as The One to meet you all over again and leads you by the heart to the crux of it all, and when you finally look into the shadows of why you hesitate, and when you come out singing to love in a raw voice—pure and bared before everything honest; what you feel next will be new and authentic and true, and fathoms deeper than any romance you've ever known.

NO ONE EVER TOLD ME
(OF THE GLORY OF GROWING OLDER)

No one told me it would be like this—
how growing older is another passage of discovery
and that aging is one grand transformation,
and if some things become torn apart
or even lost along the way,
many other means show up
to bring me closer
to the center of my heart.

No one ever told me
if whatever wonder waits ahead
is in another realm and outside of time.
But the amazement, I found,
is that the disconcerting things
within the here and now
that I stumble and trip my way through,
also lead me gracefully home.

And no one told me that I would ever see
an earth so strong and fragile, or
a world so sad and beautiful.

And I surely didn't know
I'd have all this life yet in me
or such fire inside my bones.

SOMETHING NEW

Something new is making its way to being ready.
Something fresh is finally fixing to break through.
Something old is pulling back and whispers a final blessing,
knowing it has given everything it came to give.
What was before becomes the nourishment for beginnings.
The long winter days are over.
Let the hearth's old sticks and scraps
from season's passing
be the kindling for trust and faith
to warm your imminent steps.

This has been made for you,
forming deeply within you,
this brand-new opening.

BIRTH CRY

There's a brokenness that leads to healing,
There's a sorrow that foreshadows joy.
There is beauty flowing from creation,
There's an abundance that keeps giving more.
Out of mystery arises fresh meaning.
After sleep, we awaken again.
And there's a birth cry
breaking through to the surface
when a new stage in life has begun.

GREAT FAITH

Great faith doesn't come suddenly and unexpectedly, like a powerful flash of belief lighting up the darkened sky, or all at once flowing from a staff of solid conviction and expected to part the deep waters of doubt and dissension, but from the tiny sprouts of consistent growth over time, emanating from within and brought by what others often see as failures.

Those with great faith have learned from honestly trying to do better, and keep going after botched-up attempts to succeed. Those with great faith are willing, despite being enormously afraid, to walk into a den of scorners and skeptics to render new outlooks that make ours a caring and relational world.

Those of great faith are today's giant slayers and tomorrow's bridge builders. They are super saints disguised as everyday people who've spent a lifetime on the skids of determination, cultivating intuition, honing the process of hearing clear and luminous inner-wisdom, and weaving trust, which becomes a golden brand of faith uniquely theirs. Unshakable and unmistakable.

And though their voice be heard merely as a whisper in the winds of change, their faith is continually expanding in the light of constant undertaking, strengthening each heroic attempt to step further and become wiser.

For great faith comes not out of thin air, but from the soul's deep need to endure.

OLD PAIN

No one walks through this world without tears,
a cross, or a cut that went too deep.
Without always knowing, we keep some of the past
alive in potent bottles, dusty yet sometimes
filled with charged reactivity that sabotage
our present, and labeled as Old Pain.

Old Pain in sharp responses, like doses of
early life material spilling out in our adult moments.
And Old Pain through eyes of a past event
can signify or detain the need for true healing.

Old Pain isn't who we are, rather a reference
of our tragedy and former heartache.
By moving, mending and integrating,
we begin to see through undarkened eyes.
And with a new and clearer perspective
gained through our process,
we can drink refreshing life from a fuller glass
and gaze endlessly into a wide, unclouded
and breathtaking overview.

We can live from our purest
and freshest of heart places.

THE DOORWAY
(THE SOFT AND HONEST CHAMBERS OF OUR HEART)

The doorway we walk through is the same a thousand times a day, where outside the wind feels its way through the tree branches and never really comes to know the leaves. Once, I walked inside and saw you standing there—the sunlight cast its glow upon your head and I wondered, *Why?* Why it was the softest parts were the best of us, yet what we often kept from one another. Or why there were days that pleaded we come out of hiding, and moments that begged we grow, instead we held back the beauty of our frailty, altogether.

When the silence is filled to the brim with the things we wouldn't say, when we're ravenous for the things we didn't do—I'm telling you, I never wanted it to be that way. What I want is to let you in so you can see how real I am. And all you need from me is to be brave enough to touch a beating heart that wants to bleed sheer honesty.

Maybe we can stop the undertows that keep pushing us to bury our feelings and desires. Maybe we can try to slow down time and recognize what seems twisted up and tied is our shared despair over being deprived of a recognition we secretly dream of having.

Maybe we can sit down and learn how to unwrap our needs one by one, hold them close to our bodies and give them warmth. And maybe we can keep each other safe from this day on, and protect our bond from the battered harshness of our wounding.

Maybe we can step through the doorway—see the risk, yet take the chance. Put down our shields and shed old skins. This time, lets meet the moment and speak from the soft and honest chambers of our heart.

BREAKING OPEN

Seems like it's the moments
we're stripped bare
and holding onto almost nothing,
when love dares to wake us, shape us,
and tell us to keep from wholly closing.
Maybe love will always be what keeps life going.
And life keeps going,
despite everything inside it
breaking open.

PRAYERS

What is the ultimate destination of my prayers?
The power of the mind suggests some things happen
outside my comprehension.

I imagine a prayer, once spoken, marks out its territory,
then blending with other utterances, those potent
words flow into a deeper, much wiser dimension.

And perhaps a prayer sets out in the direction
pointed, only to return in ways we may have to discern.

I know I can't push back the mist once
it begins rolling down a tree-lined mountainside.

I know the air is thick with prayers.

Mingling and rotating, always moving in every
direction, the energy from our petitions and pleadings
work together to open the floodgates of the unknown
and brings into our familiar existence,
a beacon to illuminate the path.
A beam to bridge the gap.
A wave to show us the way.

Maybe the purpose of prayer isn't to remove
us from strife, but to guide us through.

THE ART OF NOT TAKING IT PERSONALLY

The art of not taking it personally is knowing it is not about you, rather it is likely about them and their issues, which however, can disconcert when conveyed with boiling contention.

It takes practice to place your own emotional reactivity behind you as you focus on what is missing or wanting to be heard and met, but is instead strangled by the fear of being vulnerable.

To remain calm is the key when a combative struggle has seized control over words of pain, and when longings are held captive as suffering inside a wounded heart.

You must learn how to be present and ready to not fall into the trappings in which these events may attempt to pull you.

And if they persist, and begin to cost your personal peace, the great wisdom is in recognizing when to compassionately withdraw and release.

You cannot console anger or aggression.
And you will soon realize you are more
than alright knowing another person's emotional upset
belongs to them and *will not destroy you.*

LET OUR SOULS DO THE DRIVING

Let's let our souls do the driving.
Let's let our hearts do the talking.
Let's make love in tender ways
we never knew before.
Let's take down old walls and
repair misaligned doors.

Let's play in the rain, instead
of giving worry our minds.
Let's let life run the show
and be full of surprise.
Let's dream with our eyes open.
Let's fight fair with our truth.
Let's hold hands through the night,
and kiss in the stark afternoon.

Let's age as honest creatures.
Let's care for earth's children.
Let's share a blanket inside each morning.
Let's become best friends and caring lovers.
Let's spread our hearts out like angel's wings.
Let's break bread with those who feel forgotten.

Let's not argue over doctrine, but
make kindness our religion.
Let's build new roads to bring us closer
and let our souls do the driving.

ONE STAR

The stars shine to remind someone to keep going.
When the day is done and heaves its final breath
into the shadows, someone runs outside
and stretches their gaze as far as they possibly can
and tries to seize each glorious fleck of distant fire.

Someone drops to their knees and prays out loud
and desperately wishes those majestic balls of light
would hear their earthly pleading.

And with tears streaming to the ground,
someone raises their arms and spreads
determined hands all the way up to heaven.

Every night, someone is plucking one star
from that cold, dark sea and carrying
its warm flicker of hope
into the very next morning.

FAITH HEALING

When childhood wounding is hanging around adult life
peeking around corners, popping up in unexpected situations,
starving for recognition, crying out for much-needed attention,
it doesn't negate your faith to allow your redeemed soul
to work through the heavy load of early-life material.

Your faith doesn't insist you leave all your heartache
and triggers and trauma upon an alter to slip away
like faint trails of smoke.

Faith supports the entire healing journey.

It won't vow to wash away the pain, but it will
walk with you through every dark and lonely valley.

It can feel scary and unnerving
when called to enter the shadowy halls
of deep inner work.
But it's there you'll find
the very faith of God,
in the tenderest
of healing places.

TONIGHT, I WILL GO

Tonight,
I will go
to the place
deep inside
and held safe,
where there's
no worry
or regret.
No sorrow
or embarrassment.
Where it's not polluted
with panic,
resentment,
or fear.

Tonight,
I will go,
with only
the moon
and stars
and night's
fragrant perfume,
wherein
the center
of my soul
it is well.

WE ARE ALL IN TRANSITION

Will the flowers along with the trees decide to let another season by—avoid the unease of a new direction—play it safe, and not give up all they've held inside?

Even as I look for signs of what might come into view, I feel the steadfast rhythm of emergence near me, within me— around you, softly beating.

Together, we're all in transition.

Imaginings have chosen their colors. Each movement selects a time. We stand in doorways facing whatever comes with change and its perennial style. Our sisters and brothers move away, our children grow up, our parents die, yet somehow love finds us in all these places—and in all these places we find the seeds of the next experience.

Breathing in deep, exhaling slowly. Picking up the patterned pace of things, and trusting the wisdom evolving within small and constant happenings.

And every year, come spring, the leaves and petals grow in perfect time—all at once, stretching out one by one, until the lavish in each flowered crown is undeniably seen.

EVERYTHING REAL

It was never important for you to always feel special, because you were busily feeling the special in everything real. The sincerity beyond the drama. The messy. The struggle. The tension and pull. The magnificent pulsation of all things human.

You can't manage every stray moment passing by, because you're not meant to control life. Instead, intended to learn how to not hold back so often. You see, you've been ordained to be opened by it—seized at times by the grief of it all, yet still find comfort within its simplest of graces. So, even amid the thrum of routine, you can remarkably hear *everything* sing of what truly matters. To walk inside the miracle of wholeness. To welcome the thrill of small surprises. And to come awake and receive love fuller.

Life may not save you from your greatest sorrow or spare you from the fate of getting sick, losing friends, watching your child suffer, or from ever growing old. Somehow it has a way of drawing you into the full spectrum with its permeating light. Light, shining so undeniably through every circumstance, illuminating details once hidden in the depths of lived experiences.

And while life reaches out in real colors to dance with your soul, may it remind you softly:

Between the things you've endured, and must yet undergo, weaves my truest wonders. As you commit to living close to personal happenings, let me breathe in the places you feel broken and show you, there are still pleasures to be known in the pace of Everything Real.

DRIVE

We weren't meant to make the drive straight
through the night and appear before a pristine
place of quiet order and harmony the very next day.

And I didn't live up to the standard of perfection
I first thought up or that was fastened to me
years and years ago, thankfully.

Sometimes life is illegible and the way is bumpy
and confusing and awkward, lacking any
outward form of elegance or control.

We're living beings, you must know,
intended to bend and fall and grow
and keep moving within ourselves—

to be open to the depth of our process
and to honor the wonder and surprise
inside each adventurous stage
along the way.

SPIRITUAL MOTHER

Remember her as the day closes. You may have lived a life without an adoring, supportive mother, but if you look closely, maternal love has been faithfully beside you all the way. She was there for you in the stranger's kindness. She was in the wisdom of a caring friend. She was in the tender air of compassion when you needed it most. She was in your budding courage. She was in the mentors that guided you through the unknown. You learned how to trust your instincts from her teachings. She taught you how to stick to your convictions and how to believe in your dearest of dreams. She is your spiritual mother, and she has been there for you in the hearts of many others; nurturing and caring for you, reaching you in ways only a mother's love can.

Whatever season you find yourself in, there is a reason to keep living. It doesn't need to appear dramatically or look superficial. It can look like dormancy before sprouting. It can look like loving your grandchild and sharing your stories. It can be planting a seed and watching passion unfold as a rose. It's allowing the sunlight in and letting it hold you. It's knowing you still have love to give and it's not too late to receive it...

RESCUED FAITH

Do I dare to dream? Will we ever find our way out of the dense woods and into a clearing of tranquility and peace? I don't know if I'll live to see the madness of the world turn around and cultivate sensibility and truth, but I'm asking you to take my hand—then take the hand of anyone else who understands. We'll form a human chain across the darkened waters of the deep to rescue what's left of the wind tossed and tattered remnants of our aspirations and belief. Maybe it's not the end, and maybe the only choice we have is to try and make it through the longest night by doing nothing more than sticking together. Together, joined by the heart, until the morning light finds us locked in love's unwavering strength, still holding one another—clutching the rim of our rescued faith and still believing.

You write the book of earthly affirmations, every day, in your ups and downs, your struggle and strife, and in your rebounds and recoveries. You write the book of real-life inspiration. In the heat of the moment and in the firelight of victory. Every. Single. Day. You write the book.

AND THE CHILDREN WHO GREW UP

We can't easily choose to be happy, just as we could not choose our plight in childhood. Being a child of a parent who was emotionally unwell or mentally unstable, unavailable or abusive, is a shared sadness many could try, but only few would profoundly understand. Perhaps they had no choice but to automatically become the guardian. Maybe they learned they had to remain on their toes as ever vigilant. Most certainly they suffered without much deserving love and care. And the children who grew up surviving, yet found within themselves a way to feeling a true sense of healing through surrogate family, spiritual parents, therapeutic recovery, the arts, music and creation, are now the adults who transformed into everyday testaments of endurance, empowerment, and a rare brand of fiery grace. They know they must always be the primary care-giver to their precious inner-child. They get that the consequence of their early life means they will have hard days every once in a while. Intact and sitting by the edge of their path was a jewel covered with mud and dusty clay. They picked up the weathered stone and polished it into joy. These are the grown-up children who took the dirt into their own hands and forged a phenomenal path. A path that to this day, leads them to nurturing the seeds of peace and contentment, flourishing into lively, blissful flowers from inside.

WE HAD TO LEAVE HOME
(A HUMAN JOURNEY)

We had to leave home and make a human journey to understand ourselves intimately. Along the way we encountered poignant relationships that forced us to reconnect with just about every past feeling and memory stored inside the saga of ourselves. We confronted the barricades placed before each vulnerable moment and entered the tender and scary caverns of our psyches. We tangled with grief and pain, cleverly adorned in the cloak of shadow. While the beasts of all we lacked in life seemed to slither into our thoughts, at times preventing us from seeing the lambent candlelight circling the truth of our completeness. The beasts, we learned, were not meant to cause undue hardship, but to transform us.

We cradled our longings close to our soul, accepting them as our birthright, sparking desire and guiding us towards new thresholds of our own unfolding. It's been a risky expedition, but we had to leave home because we needed to step away to get a clearer view of what felt broken. What seemed lost. What felt troubling. Sometimes we even had to fall apart to uncover a deeper path inward. The only way to unlock the hidden vault and partake of the wealth streaming from healing's infinite treasure trove, we knew, was we had to leave home.

It was out there in the dust storms of life. It was there on the fertile ground of awakening. It was there in the core of our suffering that we learned to value our process and where we finally allowed ourselves to be wrapped in compassion and self-understanding. And when it was time, and with fearless minds of transfigured heroes, we set our hearts in the direction of love to come *back home*.

I SAW THE LIGHT OF MY SPIRITUAL LIFE

I saw the light of my spiritual life break the night and claim the dawning; slipping past the kitchen curtain, its ancient sunrays fill the room. With waking eyes and floating dust illuminating all around me, I lift my cup near my heart and pour a warm, earthy coffee. I carry the secrets of an entire ocean and house the wisdom of starry wonder, while the enigmas I'll never grasp mingle with the aura of a brand-new day. Inside my flesh sparks intuition and waves of distant ancestral memory, amid the drama of human conflict or the softer stirrings of an ordinary phase.

I saw the light of my spiritual life come alive beyond the twilight, within my pondering and predictions while washing the dishes from yesterday. Below all this routine, I revel in how the quiet things speak to me.

The deeper I've suffered, the more I understand others.
The longer I live, the more amazed I am to have survived.
I feel the light of my spiritual life revitalize my aging body.
The more I learn, the less I know,
filling my cup with the gifts of the morning.

LIVING FULLY

You can live life to its fullest in the ways it brings you alive. And for some, living fully isn't synonymous with a lifestyle of taking numerous trips to far away places and having a lot of extra things. It isn't about creating an impressive appearance, or even being crazy busy doing good work. It's soaking in the warmth of healthy friendships and splurging on care for yourself and others. It's saying *no* when that's the best response for you. It's understanding your worth and what that means in relationships. It's being able to show your real feelings and trusting it's okay to ask for what you need. It's allowing your fears and grief to emerge so they can speak the undeniable truth. It's desiring love and wanting to express love. It's giving and it's receiving. It's where the parts of you feel uninhibited to come out shamelessly to dance with your soul. That's the nectar of *living fully*.

ALL THE BROKEN PIECES

I say a prayer for the uncertain places;
the trying times when all I want
is to merely make it through.
The times I hurt someone I love.
The times I had to leave another.
The times I was left behind.
And the times I wasn't sure
I would completely recover.

The times I lost faith in people,
and the times it seemed no one
had an ounce of faith in me.
For the times I could not allow
myself to bend inside the water,
but froze inside of my woundedness
and could not accept the process.

For the times I didn't see the shape
of grace outlining every act and phase,
or the nourishment within each day,
but rushed to make it to the goal.
For the times when someone I care for
is dealt an unexpected blow,
and for the times I opened to allow love in,
only to let unacceptance and expectations win.

I say a prayer to remember we're in this together.
Glimpsing eternity, we are from one tree
its fallen seeds, buried under.

Taking hold and breaking open,
stretching tendrils, soft and trusting.
We're simply reaching out to each other.

I say a prayer for all the broken pieces,
that we hold to one another
and believe we'll make it,
when we lean into the supplest parts
of our reluctant, yet resilient, human hearts.

THEY COME BACK

The guilt clutching your throat
when you dared to speak up and be heard.
That shame pressing into your chest
for saying what you needed to say.
The anxiety tremoring deep inside,
flooding your nerves as you asserted
what's important to you.
Those new feelings are old feelings;
shadows of a time when you tried to claim
the consideration, love, and care every child deserves,
only to be cut off or shut down.
Old feelings that became bodily signals
coming back for you.
They come back to let you know you did the right thing
by showing up and taking your rightful place.
They come back to let you know *it's different now.*
You can own your space and you don't have to
carry the curse handed down to you
by the ones who restricted your voice
and taught you
how to fear.

INSIDE A PRAYER

The content of our prayer is more powerful than we'll ever know. Inside a prayer, our deepest confessions are revealed in complete openness and transmuted into energy. Inside a prayer is where we unfurl the immensity of our love. Inside a prayer is where we bare the human edges of our faith. Even the most secret desires of our body and soul are voiced inside our prayer. Maybe we'll never fully understand its complexities, but we swear we can feel it generating strength with every spoken word. Because prayer is the potent language of our life force, simply reaching out in intent and humbled breaths to be heard.

EVERYONE GRIEVES

Everyone grieves, but not everyone mourns. When grief becomes trapped, heavy, and much too agonizing to internalize, give yourself space to mourn. Opportunities to talk about the loss. Moments to cry and to move any tension and subsequent feelings, and ample time to rest. A fresh loss can bring up the sensations of past loss and separations, too. We all meet with loss and need to work out how to personally readjust after experiencing profound change. When grief accumulates inside, it's healthy to permit ourselves to externally mourn.

SHAPED LIKE FAITH

We learned to have faith from surviving. But we didn't survive simply to be constant markers of resilience, appointed to withstand the blunt forces of tragedies we may never fully understand. We're called by something powerful within us to find healing. To make enough sense of our path to keep going. Then we summon the strength to open one more time. And we forge the way towards letting our hearts live fully, even after something much larger outside ourselves had brought an unspeakable pain.

There's a paradox I can't describe in common language. It's been tucked inside your humblest moments of surrender, yet moves like thunder. It's something strong, something vital that's been created from the inside. It's shaped like faith and insists on being with you for the rest of your life.

MAYBE LOVE

Maybe we had an underdeveloped way of perceiving love, as we fed from the crumbs that fell at our feet and were just getting by. Maybe we gave away so much and lost touch with our worth. Maybe we never understood the importance of receiving or expressing our needs. Maybe love was never modeled to us healthily. Whatever the reasons, we are here to personally learn what it is that keeps us from fully valuing ourselves. To understand the barricades, traumas, fears, or abuses have been constraining, detaining, or shaming us from feeling loved—even as we practice trusting our hearts to open and allowing someone in.

REGRET'S PURPOSE

Then we have to go through the often-painful process of understanding and acceptance. We have to look at what is solely ours, get perspective, and put things in their proper place. We have to work through our guilt feelings because we think we haven't done enough or didn't do all the right things. Regret's purpose is not intended to haunt and harass us with blame. Regret can tell you how to make better choices. Regret can let you know its time to seek healing and recovery. Regret doesn't have to swallow you whole, but can shape you for the better before you let it go.

THE REFUGE OF HEALING

There's so much heat on healing when we don't understand its intention or its meaning. You're a human being being human. You were not meant to live out a lifetime endlessly roaming—searching for contusions to be corrected, looking for flaws to be perfected, or becoming more than what's expected. You can go on a personal journey to understand yourself and what you've been through, what comes up for you, and why certain situations trigger an individual trauma response. You can arrive at a place of feeling draped in safety, and gradually learn to trust you're not being hurt all over again. And it's this form of refuge that becomes a nurturing den. A stage to bridge the gap between injury and equanimity. A warm blanket of acceptance. Even the simplest moment of respite is what healing has in mind when it offers itself up to you...

Lean into it.
Step closer to it.
Clasp onto it.

Your growth,
your healing,
your worth.

WHAT'S AMAZING ABOUT GRACE

What's amazing about grace, is how it speaks
in the center of inconspicuous and fallible moments.
It speaks through the healer, the sick one and teacher.
It's in the presence of an ancestor, a child or a season.
Inside the flash of a memory, and through a feeling of peace.

Unwinged and in need,
we're bestowed the purest gift to fill
the cracks and line the wear and tear
of our frail and earthly garments.
Grace appears to restore and assist us,
to strengthen and enrich us.

What's amazing about grace
is that it appears as a guide,
meeting us exactly where we are,
to walk us through.

Letting go is hard because it involves a
change we are not completely prepared
to make, or allowing for a yes when we
are not ready to consent. And there are times
when it requires a process before you're ready
and journey to get to the altar of *letting go*.

WHAT A POET COLLECTS

Old photos and memories and thoughts to reflect;
these are some things a poet collects.
Dried petals, weathered stones, lost dreams and regrets.
Glass jars of nostalgia and summer sunsets.

Wisdom and wit, broken lines indirect
are a few other things a poet collects.
Blue hours when evening and dawn intersect.
Discarded wishes and feelings unchecked.

The whimsy and notions other people reject,
are a couple more things a poet collects.
Recapture, rekindle, rebirth and refine
are some things that a poet will do with their time.

Imagery, simile, free verse and lyric
are woven as cloth by the poet mystic.
Patterns and metaphor set to rhythm sublime,
as the human condition is wrought into rhyme.

There's a hush in the air when peace lands in the soul.
There's a grace released when the truth unfolds.
There's a sense of relief when a story gets told.
And there's a way with words only the poet knows.

WHEN LOVE TAUGHT US

After all is said and done,
will you know how much you meant,
did you love and allow love in,
and did you shelter the lives of the innocent?

The ancient stirrings of the heart
that swept us out from our primal caverns of isolation
and into the tender arms of belonging
are still with us in the darkened hours.

And the night we fear calls us back
to the early light of our beginning,
when we learned to open and be welcoming,

and when love taught us
how to survive
by burning a fire beyond our caves
called *human care*.

A HEARTBEAT AWAY

You're just a heartbeat away from the caring hands of healing, the strong arms of believing, and the nourishment of good friends. You're just a heartbeat away from the vast seas of freedom, the peacefulness of evening, and the sustenance from within. Your life has real meaning in the midst of uncertainty, in the rains of calamity, and in the deep throes of pain. The essence of life pulsates inside you like an ancient drum, thrumming stories from its hold, pumping strength in its blood—supporting everything in its rhythm that has ever been before, giving breath to your dreams, carrying hope in its veins. Don't be swept by the cold waves of darkness or from empty worries be withdrawn. You're just a heartbeat away from a love without end.

AN OLD STONE TURNING

I can say with sincerity, I have been here before. I have known enough suffering to recognize it in another's weary eyes. I have felt the qualms of fearing what the next day will reveal. I've been swallowed by waves of insecurity in feeling I'll not be enough. I have lived through the apprehension of another hurdle set before me. Although you don't deserve it, and there's no valid answer to offer why the good must undergo the deepest pain, I know without a doubt you'll rise again. There's an old stone turning. There is a cycle coming to a close. You will make it through tomorrow, you will be enough for one day to hold.

RECLAMATION

We lose so much in one lifespan. Our possessions become destroyed. Our home is left behind. We lose our voice to years of ongoing distress. We've lost our renderings, inspired lines, and the many transcriptions along the way. Old journals and photos. Faded ribbons and clippings, and even the key items that have surprisingly influenced our identity. The things we really needed, the gatherings of being human. Clothes and tools and all the emotional investments are washed away by the floods of time.

For some, there is a moment. A point of letting go of everything they thought they knew about having. Somehow, they release what they once believed was the only way to be, to embrace yet another.

I tell you, those who lost their way will own their path again. They will speak with authority once more, those who've been grieving the precious power of personal expression. Those who've been driven from shelter will collect the seeds of a new phase and grow another beginning. And know this, the things that could never become lost are truly prized. For those who kept them embryonically safe inside, a clear and mighty birth cry will be heard as a memorable fresh page is written into life.

WHEN EVERYTHING GOOD IS GONE

Friend, you might reach the harsh edges of time that only appear inside a certain age, or upon an inevitable season, when it seems everything good is gone. When you feel like there is no beauty left in your eyes, no admiration for your soul. No strength left to try, no more innocence to hold. And you think you now see the world how it really is.

In these vacillating times when grief is ambiguous or when sadness foregrounds this kind of suffering, when the dawn is jaded and when the loveliest of flowers has paled, may I see beauty outside of beauty and hope within hopelessness. Show me the promise inside difficulty and lead me to comfort after pain.

And while this loss is a clouded sky that I can't see through nor understand, guide my eyes to other people in real situations that can use a caring hand. Awaken my sleeping senses to the vison born inside a simple morning; fill the air with faithful birdsong and belief for overcoming. Give me the laughter of a child and a hunger in my spirit, then remind me once again:

Everyone struggling to become is a thing of beauty in this world.

When it seems the best of me is spent and I can't give back any longer, open my heart a little wider that I might take the purest breaths of love inside each life-given moment.

THE NATURE OF LOVE AND WOUNDING

There finally came a day when we who were injured by human connections had to trek back to the outpost of painful experiences coiling in our memories to begin the process of unlearning what we thought was love.

When we did something right, we gained acceptance, approval and adoration. If we did something not quite right, we may have encountered subsequent guilt, shame and frustration.

So, we began to condition our self to receive the warmer responses. We went as far as to adjust our behaviors, our expression, and even our precious trying—something necessary to develop healthily.

Some of us may have become *less than* in order to savor that crucially important component to feeling happy and alive. To exist fully embraced by care and attention.

What we came away with, instead, would be our confused ideas based on set patterns established to survive a relationship. Tenderness, approval and even affection, all granted on certain terms.

Did you learn to make someone feel good so you might, in turn, feel good about being you? And perhaps you finally caught on to the fact that all these motives had nothing to do with giving and receiving authentic love. Rather, they're the conduct of those trapped in abuses, shackled by trauma, and controlled by their own cycle of wounding.

You made the journey backtracking the thicket of a
bewildering past and separated from the chaos. You
no longer need to be afraid of opening to the sunshine
genuinely nurturing your blossoming soul. Now you know,
love is not our wounding. Not our skewed behaviors brought
on by childhood trauma. Not our twisted beliefs based on
surviving a previous relationship.

Love is a grace leading us away from confusion and torment
and into the warmth of softness and understanding. When
it draws near, you will know to trust it, dear heart.

OUNCE OF HOPE

Bring your ounce of hope, your remnants of faith, and leave what's left of your fear. Because in the end, it's what you carry inside your heart that will close the gap, override the divide, and piece together what's been severed. You may think you're but a mere voice speaking into the whirlwinds of a world overtaken by terror and storm, but if you have kindness, mercy and grace, you possess a power called love that will crush the borders of hate.

STEP QUIETLY

Step quietly over the doorsill into the room and don't
be afraid. Though it seems you're the only one walking
through the vale of darkness on a daily basis. Though it's
true you may be the one living hourly with illness or disease.
Though it's you whose breath may be drawing ever closer to
timelessness. Whatever it is that's been frightening for you,
know you are consecrated by an all-seeing love. It is a love
that shelters and sustains, dwelling within—wherever
you are, come what may. A love which transcends life's
most compelling questions and understands every nuance
of the complicated mind. A love that has melded over the
years with your gifts, and has been woven into the care you
brought to nourish a hungry world. It has shaped itself into
a quilted shawl and now wraps around you as an aura of
light. Let it absorb the shadows, let it warm your trembling
heart, and let it comfort any unease you are holding.

A FINGERPRINT

Personal trauma is much like an individual fingerprint. We can't command everyone to recover within the same amount of time. We can't expect to fasten the exact remedy onto each one in the hopes they will heal or lock into the stages of recovery. The aftershocks of tragedy can be an avalanche of helplessness and distress, often burrowing. Sometimes festering. Always managing a way to break the surface. If only we could really see the tender spaces they move through in their everyday. If only we could remember their mortality and consider how often they must reach for an ointment to allay the pain. We might see with our own eyes they are doing what is just right for them. We might see their efforts look like courage. We would see their healing takes its own time and requires patience. And we would know every soul walks an original path where no one else has ever been before. A path that responds to kindness. A path extending kindness, in turn, to those who walk beside carrying a bundle of heartbreak of their own.

GOLDEN BRIDGE

Did you know you're allowed to cherish your entire life as a process shamelessly? Each bumpy, awkward experience and every single creamy, effortless moment within your individual chapter of development. This is not a mad dash for excellence, nor a race to see if you can get it all right by age thirty-two. Over time, you will find new purpose being in your forties, love inside your fifties, sensuality in your sixties, and tireless dreams waking into existence all throughout. However long you're alive, there is a phase, a stage, a setback, and an opening to find a new lens. A gate to enter a deeper realm inside your soul. A chance to find another golden bridge to cross. Everything is here for you and willing to become a part of solving the mystery of who you are and why you're here.

TOUR DE FORCE

What if you didn't make it to the front of the line,
finish the marathon, or beat the crowd?
What if you didn't inspire vast ripples on the web,
go viral with your gospel, or create new cyber trends?

What if you didn't learn to speak another language,
drive a car across country, or blossom into a true-blue yogi?
What if you didn't use more time to just listen,
be still and reflect, or simply hold out your hand?

What if you didn't permit yourself passion,
take one more chance, or allow yourself to be seen?
What if you didn't give heed to your heart,
feed all those fears, or walk boldly through that door?

You will develop in each season
to ripen wholly into your prime.
So what does it matter, the things
you didn't do in this allotted time,
when the tour de force is within
every treasured moment
you cup your worthwhile life
inside the love of your hands
to kiss full on the mouth,
all its cherished wonder.

THE PULL OF YOUR CALLING

There's a gravitational pull happening between your soul and what it calls out for you to do. There are times it implores you to soak yourself inside this one and only thing until it feels satisfied. There are times it needs a season, and nothing more. There are situations where it demands a lifetime.

Do whatever your calling looks like.

Everyone has heard its plea, whether it's loving a child into adulthood or guarding the trees, or becoming an artist or practicing as a servant leader. Only you are privy to its vision, and only you can recognize its voice when it speaks to you.

FEELING USED

Strangely, in the absence of recognition you might feel both useless and used. Like a cloth worn from giving, with no sense of meaning or worth outside its purpose. With the lack of appreciation, often the only thing to do is to remind them you're human and need care and thanks, too. And if that doesn't shift the reality to remedy the hollowing feelings breeding inside, it may be time to correct your surroundings. It may mean you have to prevent yourself from doing things for people who overlook your valuable energy, expecting you to produce immediate results. It may mean you have to set the boundaries. It may mean you have to say *No*. It may mean you have to leave them until they understand your importance in their lives. It may mean you might not ever hear from them again...

ON THIS MORNING

There's a whispering in the woods and if you're silent you can hear its secrets. If you're still, you can feel your heart beat among the sages. When you're seeking, the trees become the scriptures that open wide its pages to offer meaning.

So much time spent answering phones, responding to texts and scrolling a list of endless messages, pushing away the real questions whose only intention is to let you come out of the hard shell you've been curled up inside and what you call a life:

On this morning, I come to witness the miracle of light filtering through the branches, illuminating inside of me all the niggling indecision I needed to bury or ignore to buy myself time:

Can you be with this? Can you let go of that?
And can you endure the discomfort of not knowing?

You have to walk a while before you get to the woods and before the trees bow down to become a passageway you can't avoid anymore. But when you get there, you can unfold into your natural state as all the thoughts that were placed in hiding come out to gather at the feet of something grand and telling.

CHILDLIKE FAITH

I want always to enjoy a childlike faith,
one not found in the ways of those who claim
every set belief is immovable,
or where nothing inquisitive can ever
rise from the floor.

I want a faith that finds itself
skipping from one curiosity
to the next, gleefully declaring
the wonder before my eyes
and forever asking,
How does this happen?
What does it all mean?
Can this be real...and why?

I want a tender faith
that doesn't settle for less,
instead eagerly searches
the unknown places
for what's uncertain
and discovers bits of truth
inside hide-and-seek rooms.

A faith that allows my intrigue to bloom—
and where I candidly explore
open halls and dynamic ideas.
I want a growing faith
stretching out in my mind,
encouraging my trust
to believe in so much more.

ANOTHER SEED

We nurture our hopes and tend to the fire inside our dreams in the best ways we know. Our earnest of dreams, despite a sense they've withered away into faded passion, are surprisingly resilient.

Sometimes we let ourselves be stopped by the rain storms that drown and wash away the only home we thought we ever had. The only place we thought were stored our most prized and secret visions.

Yet, in another way—from another place, from another seed, perhaps—a dream can break through the struggle, seize the light, and flourish in full and vibrant colors as it comes alive.

BLENDED PRAYERS

I stand on the brink of evening's shadow,
the sunlight hours far away, now worlds apart.
I pour my prayers into the vast and open sky
to meet with yours and be entwined.

They lace with grace before they fuse
with the horizon's gentle hues.
I sense the earth is tense with whirling worry,
reaching out to heaven for calm release.

What's to become of dawn and dreams and life
when uncertain times overshadow truth, I do not know.
For now, tonight may our blended prayers
serve to unite as love knits us close with
the peaceful yearnings of our heart.

THE LENS OF LOSS

Grief can seem
not like an interval
of sorrow, but more like a lens.
A lens in which the details
of everything appear as distorted,
or even magnified.
Mornings, comments,
possessions, sunsets
and shorelines have an altered
look to them now.
Numbness, anger, sadness
and despair become the new prayers
quietly uttered and cried amid
the motions of normality.
There is no going back to before,
but to go on, because the frailest
of things keep living.
So you continue and go on,
yet hold close the haunting beauty
of each memory
as if they were a cloth
you've wrapped to keep in place
an enduring but injured heart.

SLOW MOTIONS

On the way to getting there,
I found a powerful place taking an unhurried pace,
with small steps close to the ground,
my soles mesh with the great stepping stones
of patience, acceptance, gratitude and grace.

Slowing down, I could breathe deeper into my hands
and touch each gradation of my sadness
and appreciate loss as a perspective
of what was, cherished or unwanted,
and perceive my attachment to all of it.

Taking it slow, I could drop in and listen to the pain
inside my anger or feel the euphoria of being in love,
and appreciate in new light how I really can't
conjure up thankfulness to wear as a banner,

instead trust it's sweeter to wait and be still.
To deliberate and lay open, like an ocean strand,
then be drenched by the unpredictable waves
of gratefulness rushing through me.

In my own time, I am a sentient being,
mingling with the seasons inside me,
churning softly and freely, making a
slow-burning love to my soul.

THE TEACHER

A seasoned teacher welcomes the struggle with understanding and patience. They recognize in order to learn; one must grasp and assimilate with space and time. The teacher apprehends the lifelong unfolding of transforming material as metamorphic, thoughtfully allowing for information to be exchanged, then swirl and eddy before settling in as illuminating knowledge. Yes, they are sensitive to opportunities for expansion and give way to the sometimes-awkward process of learning.

The teacher appreciates the necessity of reflection and practice being leaders of experience. They are receptive to the learner landing on wrong impressions as the way to meaningful realizations.

I thought it was this way,
but instead I can see it in this light...

How great the teacher who knows that for them it's not a lone journey, rather a sacred odyssey across complicated and worthwhile terrain where together we access God within, and how inside a single molecule are a million revelations.

A teacher's work is ceaseless.
So bless the great teacher.
Forever bless the life student.
For as long as we live,
we all must keep learning.

THE PERFECT STATE OF HAPPY

Along the way you might encounter a person who'll say, you're not happy, their words spewed out as a put-down, or felt much like an accusation rather than concern. As if you have failed to optimize your life in exemplar ways. As if you mismanaged your circumstances. They may not even consider, most likely, how you work at navigating complex waters in order to stay afloat on the rapids of life. They may go on to harshly judge or critique your performance, as if your personal efforts to succeed should meet a perfect picture of real accomplishment.

As if, as if, *as if.* Don't listen to them. Self-actualization is an ongoing process. Life holds in it, an active sequence of events. Respect your experiences. If you feel dissatisfaction, it's yours to own and possess as your inner-prompting guides you to identify and evaluate what's required to create special change. A change which allows you to develop further and meet with joy.

There are places inside each place. There are pastures next to fields. *Becoming* is a series of fertile sets, each set explored, grazed, and cultivated in its separate time and space.

All the elements required for our evolution are held within our existence and stem outward, unfolding and maturing through lived encounters. We discover an honorable form of contentment is present when we feel we're on our way to (or at) our personal peak, and when we accept whatever that looks like.

And even while we think we're not standing in a moment of utter bliss, sometimes we are where we need to be, wearing the soft glow of promise and any trace of individual fulfillment we organized in the grasslands of our reality, and not found inside another person's idea of the perfect state of happy.

I TRULY AM

Who we are to ourselves matters greatly, our sense
of identity an ongoing and underlying need.

In the course of living, we try many things and
shed the skins of many blunders.

Yet, anything we once were,
and everything we tried in the process,
becomes the nourishment that makes us
even more.

And so, there are times I stand in the dirt
of all I've tried to be and feel vibrant
and alive—even with the pouring rain
washing over me, again and again.

And all over again.

Because the beauty of all I am becoming
sprouts from the soil of every loss
that came from trying,
and from each assurance I believe,

and all the things I know
without a doubt,
I truly am.

RESILIENCE IS BORN

And the things
that didn't break inside
are yet within
your heart alive—
strong enough to hold,
plenty brave to endure,
patient to withstand
—as sacred provisions
to see you through.

Resilience is born
out of all you've survived.

The reality is, not everyone can transform their deep sadness or depression into gold and that's okay. If a shapeless shadow has been following you around throughout life, or comes in unsuspecting waves to engulf you when you least feel capable of managing it, please know you are not alone or in any way defective. You don't have to be an alchemist when you can be completely human. You don't need to hide your suffering from the ones who truly care.

KINDNESS IS AN OASIS

Kindness chose not to belittle,
be indifferent or cruel,
but was found in the tender curves of a smile.
In the softened tones of expression.
In the hand that reaches deep or extends itself
to care, without expecting anything in return.

When the world feels harsh,
there is a lush green spot in the middle
of a parched desert.
Kindness is an oasis where the faint of heart
can be renewed and where the merest
trickle of mercy allays the suffering.

Let kindness be your daily ritual.
Let it flow from the wellspring of your heart.

HONEST AGING

The beautiful thing about growing older is that we don't have to defy or deny age by expecting it to be just like another decade, or insisting it's a mere number, or proclaiming it to be *the new something*. Honest aging will gracefully announce another layer, another truth, another pain or new pleasure, another wisdom, another wrinkle and even another dream or possibility.

RADIANT

There are storms that will demand
every ounce of your inner strength.
There are moments that will entice
the core of your integrity.
There are oppositions that will test your resolve.
There are trials that will shake
the ground around feeling *enough*.
And there are voyages that will obscure
your very sense of belonging.

So, when you see yourself in any of these—

in the fire seeping through the narrow crack,
or in the beam escaping the folds of a dark curtain,
and in the golden streaks breaking past the narrow trees,

—know that I see you, too.

You are a star giving birth to such radiant
light by its own miraculous energy.

A MILLION SHINING CYMBALS

The aging winds
of autumn
slips through
my window
in one breath,
I think of you
as the curtains
start to tremble.

Looking up
at the moon
rich with
scintillating embers,
your name
rises from my lungs
once again in a song.

And everything I feel tonight
blends with the air—

then the stars
chime in,

like a million
shining cymbals.

ANOTHER PEACEFUL MORNING

Peace isn't something that wondrously appears like the dawn of a beautiful morning, instead it's something we must make together in these the toughest days we may have ever seen. Peace takes time to build and shape and definitely requires caring hearts and hands of patience. The thunder rolls and conflict fires across the vast and open prairie. We are afraid and uncertain and swear we must be losing all the serenity and stability we believed we truly had. We feel threatened as we watch with wide eyes cast upon a treacherous sea, fear swelling inside our bellies, as though everything we knew before surfaces to be tossed about, surging and breaking inside each turbulent wave. We are being tried and we are being tested by our times, there is no doubt. We are here together to recreate a new dawn. We are here to weave justice into tomorrow. We will show up with willing hands to build a compassionate understanding. And together we will see another peaceful morning.

CURRENT

Sometimes the truth is intense and unencumbered when it
arrives, and like a rushing current, overtakes the mud and
every obstruction in its path, and our receptiveness to meet
it is equally invested and matching in power.

And then there are times when the truth wafts in like a
hushed wind. An ever-subtle shift in another direction, but
its impact is just as potent and sure.

Like in that infinitesimal moment when a cut stops hurting
and starts healing. Or like the day you will never forget
for as long as you live, when before a mirror you stood and
searched for any illuminating signs of life—questioning, *had
you lost yourself entirely, or had you merely forgotten who you
really are?*

And the realization surged through like a current, how the
role you'd been trying to play for others never felt genuine,
instead it's been wearing you down, dulling your senses, and
grating against the protective bones of your soul.

Leaning in, the weight of your heart dropped below the
surface to dismantle the parts and pieces you had to put out
and supply to get by,

then more questions began to rumble and burn their way
out into the open. Questions that refuse any longer to be
damned behind a wall inside. Questions that might tear up
the ground around you. Questions whose sole promise is to

respond with brutal truth, but hold the only answers that will bring you back to life.

FOOTFALL

When it feels as if you're being pressured
and pushed to put it in gear, hurry up,
life is short and expectations are unending,

in the feverish haste,
in the demanding mind trip
of living with all burners set on high,
love your soul tenderly slow
in the rush of your surroundings.

Breathe in deeply and exhale slowly.
No one can control your breaths,
your movements, your pace.

You own the footsteps
that carry you down the path
of your soul's calling

and determine the speed
that brings a special
value to life—
the colors, the auras,
the desirable haven, the sound
of your own footfall.

They can wait.
It can wait.

LIFE HAS A GREATER PLAN

How long have you been in prison for it? How many times have you played it on repeat, singing along with the heartbreak of living inside the consequence of a past action? And how often have you heard, *just let it go* or *get over it*?

If it were this easy, more people would not be incarcerated by regret. Few would allow themselves to remain as captives of remorse for such a long time. Letting go is often a process over time that will vary individually. For some, it has taken years to reconcile with a single decision they once made, while others remain locked away in an existence of self-inflicted punishment.

But that's not life-affirming behavior. Because life is not in the business of handing out a never-ending sentence of bread and water with a routine serving of self-loathing. Life has a greater plan which asks you to recall—had you a better, clearer option available at the time, you would have reached for it with ease.

Now life invites you to evolve. To examine the situation. To take a closer look at what the *It* is, and to learn and grow from what you call a mistake. As painful as it feels, growth is essential for any living being to advance. And mistakes are part of the process.

So when you are ready, take it all in, then try once again. Walk through the door. You can forgive yourself, finally, and let life flow.

AN EVERYDAY AWAKENING

Inside the smallest
of moments
are the greatest
life instructions.
In the flower's blossom
there is a vibrant guide.
I am, at times, the student.
To another, I am the teacher.
Like the continual seasons,
life is an ongoing lesson,
where I may ask and learn
along the way,
peeling apart the petaled
layers of an everyday
awakening.

BREATHE

What's got you by the throat?
What has you catching a breath,
swallowing whole your feelings,
and clenching your soul?
What couldn't you say
because you were told long ago,
pull yourself together
and keep going.
Your fright.
Your worry.
Your anxiousness
and hurry.
Gas on the right.
Brake on the left.
No standing.
No stopping.
Stay on the run.
Stuff it down,
no time to feel it—
sensation has no place
while there's work to be done.

Let it lay where it was thrown,
to stifle coughs and gasp for air.
Just. Keep. Moving.

And all you want
is to catch up to yourself
and b r e a t h e.

LIVING IN YOUR BODY

Living in your body doesn't imply you've figured out how to feel good or to sustain it. Living in your body means not only accepting, but embracing and, yes, even loving its limitations. Living in your body means acknowledging what comes up for you, and being involved with what's happening to you in the moment. Living in your body means recognizing the trauma it may have undergone, or the storms it may have weathered to get you through the past. You survived the impact. Shallow breaths did their part to detain your feelings for protection. Rigidity was an armor that kept you alive. When you feel safe, allow your deep and true breaths to bring you into a full and authentic connection with the aftermath. Reclaim your body and show life you are really here for it.

Stop. Breathe in.
Feel honestly. Breathe out.
Keep breathing.

Your body still holds the experience.
Let your breaths open wide your lungs
and belly to pour out the contents.

Look at it. Examine it. Talk to it.
Shout at it. Cry for it, thank it.
Keep breathing.

Loosen your hold on whatever waves and washes through.
Feel as your saving breath vocalizes those once receded
emotions as released.

IT'S EASY TO LOVE

It's easy to love when it's love
that's being given. It's easier to give
when there's something to have.

But what a daring thing it is to open
every soft, selfless chamber of your heart
and start giving—even as you stand bared
in the bitter air of the unknown.

Will you be received? Will your care be spurned?
Will your love be ignored? What happens in the end?

You can drive all night, you can search the land,
you can plead with the stars, and you can hold out
for something you've only dreamed of that can
fill your cup of endless longing.

Or,
you can be still and look in the places
where there's no sweet music,
no seductive lighting,
no pledges to be the one—
where only the thirst for urgent answers thrive,
and listen for the faint hunger cries,

then open up your heart
and let your love pour,
and help fill the empty stomach
of a famished world.

GLIMMERING HOPE

When the night
collapses
into its bleakest places,
I look to the stars
huddling closely—
glimmering
in the dark
to signal
hope.

THE RESURRECTION FERN

It felt like everything died inside.
Everything burned like fire,
all the energy you had—
now spent and rests crumbled
in a lifeless pile upon the floor.
Yet, when another rain transpired,
another wind revived,
the resurrection fern you are,
came back to life
and surprised the world.

SURRENDERING

Like a tree giving up its bounty, letting go for want of something even more. Not second guessing every motion. Not seeing what comes next. Not feeding the need to always know. And you didn't see with clarity, the very end of each progression, or what would transpire each time you said yes to change.

To make the next move sometimes meant letting go of something long-standing in the process. You didn't know the exact outcome of what would happen if you exchanged security for the more gratifying job. Or leave a familiar place to take a bold step closer in a relationship. Or had the serious conversation that might challenge a friendship, shake up a lifeless dynamic, or possibly end a marriage. Each step-in transition requires decisions, plus, an element of yielding to the unknown. Before each conclusion was a struggle. You decide to give a little more of yourself and loosened your hold of something else.

And the tree won't back out of its inevitable transformation because the certainty of loss, but gives way to the surprise of what might be born, instead. We don't get to see how it'll be in the end, but we trust our hearts find the way. We're like that sometimes. Like everything in nature. Surrendering, without fully knowing.

ABANDONMENT

We each, at one time
or another, fall into
a ditch we dug ourselves
and can't easily climb
our way out, see the light,
or make it right again.

Not always can anything
instantly be done, except
to stay close through
the coldest hours of
the lonely night and build
a warm fire.

I always felt, a soft abiding
presence caresses the soul
to say we're not alone,
and is the counteracting agent
to the ultimate dark hole we fear
called *abandonment*.

PAINTED LADY
(TAKE TIME TO LIVE)

How long has it been since your last confession? When
was the last moment you admitted your worth and
reconciled with your mind? Have you been creating a life, or
responding to circumstances? Survival know-how compels
you to function and move, but I wonder where you've been
keeping yourself these days. Somewhere in the blur, there
you are. Won't you come out for a while and take time into
your reflections, into your movements, your desires? Time
has a sweet spot waiting for you, breathing all its color and
fragrance into every organic thing.

Take time to plant a seed and watch something grow. And
do you know how long a painted lady lives? Take time to
watch her single life clear from silk cocoon until she breaks
through with stained-glass wings—then from flower to
flower, she tells her life story.

Take time to tend a garden. Walk the shoreline.
Touch the moss. To be with your dreams.
Take time to see yourself with kinder eyes.
Take time to make peace with your heart.
Take time to bathe in the fragrance of lilac, just bloomed,
and savor the earthy scent of the ground while it rains.
Take time to give bread to your body, drink in the sunlight
and bathe with the trees. Take time to be nurtured. To taste.
To see. Eat plentifully from the soul food time willingly
brings.

POETRY SAYS YES

Poetry says *yes*, you can come indoors
and talk about anything that compels you.

Poetry says *yes*, you can enter its realm
and language your true sensations.

Poetry says *yes*, you can step outside
their rules to unearth and invent your own expressions.

Poetry says *yes*, you can open wide and take
up space to convey your private feelings.

Poetry says *yes*, you can.

THIS ONE LIFE

This one life. So full of
things true and untrue,
and pieces holding
elements of both.

You were not born to sit
remote in one place
and watch from a window,
the days pass into
seasons, holding on
to what was probably never yours
—but to step through
the doorway.

To go outside
to feel the vitality of each season.
To be surprised and feel refreshed.
To align with what feels true
inside this space in time.
And to be warmed
by the beams of love,
even while you try
to put it all together
—somewhere,
inside.

I'M HOLDING OUT FOR DRIFTWOOD

What if I were to allow you close enough to read the lines written on my skin—or tell you even, how my prized secrets are really rustic yearnings? For, unlike those who want for instant gain or trivial things, I come seeking for only what time and life can bring. Like evenings of soaking the sunset into my body until my bones memorize every subtle meaning in soft colors. Or listening to the howling wind as it sweeps across my sinewy limbs. And watching the distant whitecaps collide—recalling how I lived to be stripped bare and ride with the breeze, yet hold the past, present and future as the riches of eternity.

You'd find, between birth and death I move and breathe, from the forest to the earnest sea. By peaks and crests I become refined—shaped by waves, smoothed by time. Broke apart, then purified by the gift of life's transforming fire. Then I'd tell you how I wait on those who are just like me; who bear the scars just as they are. And like the rugged beauty of mystery, we are the wonderment of profoundly more. And how I look for little signs of something deeper in the working. How I'm standing by with the turning tides, and while I'm held by the tender hands of sand, I'll wait for the worthwhile to appear unplanned.

I'm holding out for driftwood.

Because like driftwood, the smallest wonders offer the greatest reassurance that everything I'm becoming and everything I'm here for, in its time, wastes no time to gently wash ashore.

CROSS SEA

Life is a cross sea of waves and currents,
forcing us this way and that,
pushing and pulling us
over and under,
stretching us out,
filling us with questions—
making us wonder,
what will become of us
in the end?

The force of life is real.
The struggle to keep going
is raw and certain.
The challenge to be here
so palpable, at times.

Yet, in the midst of our most grueling hardships,
sometimes what becomes our greatest hope
is not for everything to turn out perfectly,

but that we come to understand
the meaning of however
it
turns out to be.

CREATIVITY

If I'd waited until I was a flawless artist,
I would not have let my spirit soar across
the sky in raptured colors.

If I had waited to become the most elegantly poised,
I would not have let my feet leap beside my soul
to dance inside the starry cosmos.

What can hold us up is our holding out.

Waiting for the perfect time.
Hoping to be better.
Listening to belittling voices.
Thinking you are alone.

Creativity cries out in the dark
to wake you up and take hold of it.
To be in it. Sway to it.
Play with it. Never be freed of it.
And let it pull you along for the rest of your life,
calling your name exhaustively.

Because creativity, once lit, burns inside
like a deep, deep need.

RISK

Leaving the only home
I've ever known
to build a new one.
Knowing I'll be unearthed,
my spirit tried,
my tears will spill into
a cleansing river,
when choosing to say yes
to transformation.
Welcoming the morning,
the lesson,
the birdsong,
the connection,
says *I'm open*,
I'm willing—
let my heart expand,
let me honor the broadening
of my story.

And the things I risk to hold,
but bring me back to life,

and the ways I risk to grow
to reveal the nature of my soul,

become the evidence,
the signposts,
telling me I'm home.

WHEN YOU'RE FREE TO BE YOU

When you risked bringing
your authenticity out into the open,
despite the possibility of being shut down,
unliked, judged as reckless and ridiculous,
or even ignored entirely,
I want you to know, I felt you.
I can see it's not something you can do
all the time around everyone, yet.
I want you to take in how much courage it took
to put yourself out there
in the face of potential shaming and danger.
I want you to believe in your truth
and feel unequivocally supported when you present it.
Because there's nothing more liberating
than doing what your heart has been aching for.
And there's nothing more powerful
than when you're free to be *you*.

DOORS

Doors close all the time.
Disappointments arise.
Walls go up
and connections dissolve.

When I feel left out,
let me allow love in.

Let me open a window
and look out to remember,
I am part of a family that cares.

And when what I long for
doesn't come through,
let me look beyond the shadows for joy.
Let me see sunbeams streaming through
the leaves of the unexpected and unnoticed.
Let me listen for the softest of invitations
to open my heart,
to step across
the threshold
where waits the discovery
of so much more.

FOR ALL MY *DIDN'TS*

For when I didn't fully live each moment
or deeply relish my precious time.

For when I didn't seize the day
or respond to 'life is passing by'.

For when I didn't dare to dream
or let potential maximize.

For when I didn't come out and risk,
but stayed inside and hid.

For when I didn't see the meaning
or get the lesson in each teaching.

For all my *didn'ts* are held in love,
just as much as all my *dids*.

I thought I was climbing, turns out I'm the mountain.
I thought I was flying, but I was the sky all along.
I'm not the sun or the stars, I'm the cosmos surrounding.
I am not a lone voice, I'm an entire song.

NOW YOU CAN SAY *THANK YOU*

You had to be brilliant to make it through. You needed to be clever, insightful and swift. Your guise was your handiwork. Your creation. At times it was a life preserver. There were moments and places when you needed to craft a quick façade to withstand your discomfort. Now you can witness the necessary pretext you devised in those times with absolutely no judgement. Now you can tenderly cup the face you needed to present to the world being spread out before you and say *thank you*.

DANDELION WISHES

How many wishes had the dandelions heard
before one turned around and whispered back
to her the secrets of her worth:

The beauty of a flower is held inside the promise of a seed,
and the world within you holds the same promises.

EACH NOBLE STEP

No more fawning to diffuse conflict.
No more shifting your presence to please,
appease, and just get through the situation one more time.
No more taking responsibility for the negative behaviors
of other people, or emotionally checking out on yourself
to accommodate everyone else.

It is a process.
It may require support.
And it takes time, awareness, and care to boundary
and balance within and take sovereignty
of your own internal territory,
where each noble step brings you closer
to coming home to you,
the beloved.

RECOMMENCE

Getting on with your life and not reliving the heartache
of what you were never given—after the healing work,
grieving your losses, and creating a nurturing inner parent
—means you don't have to keep absorbing the pain.
It means no longer sitting inside what
didn't transpire, hedged in aloneness.
You don't have to do without anymore,
inhabiting the outskirts of your existence,
tangled in regrets, slowly dying of loneliness,
serving what never appeared.
You can treat yourself to kindnesses.
You can be nurtured by what inspires you.
You can show up for yourself and be open
to authentic experiences.
You are here for it fully now,
and can feed from the abundance
of real intimacies.

HOLDING SPACE

I won't try to fix your problem,
I won't cover you in toxic light.
I'm not here to give away free wisdoms
or weigh you down with my hard-luck stories,
because it's not a competition.

When all you need right now is presence,
I can hold you safe and tight.
I'll be a quiet strength who's sitting vigil,
and if you want to pour your heart out,
I will not judge, but deeply listen.

THE PAST LIVES OF *NOT ENOUGH*

Don't inhabit for too long
the past lives of *not enough*.

Don't roam endlessly inside
the ghost town of a soulless connection,
or stay locked away in
an empty room after they leave.

And when you come out of the shadows
of what's never been possible,
come live inside the vast and luscious lands
of a fertile life that's been ready, willing,
and genuinely wanting to meet with you
more than half-way.

SILENT BRAVERIES

Sometimes it takes looking
at your struggles to recognize
the depth of your courage.
To be in awe of what it takes
to face real fears,
break old patterns,
and climb the steep ridges
of your own private mountain.
Even the silent braveries
carried out over time
cover the ground
all around you.

NEW EYES

When we find new eyes, we might have to break our own hearts in life. We might have to look at situations square in the face using these fresh new eyes. Eyes that see through our most salient fantasies and identify the ones holding information about our core wounding and the ones clasping our earliest of primal needs. With these new eyes we have to examine our idealizations—why we created them and why they can't hold up over the long haul. We risk recognizing what's unsustainable or weighing us down and holding us back in our journey. With these new eyes, we have to redirect our inner focus towards letting go of what doesn't work in reality or what's continually hurting us. New eyes might make us have to walk away from harmful environments and foggy relationships if we want a loving, sound and peaceful existence. Our new eyes are the seers who recognize our behavior is the only controllable option under the circumstances. Yes, waking up to new eyes isn't always an easy, breezy experience. Because these new, awakened eyes might lead us to a time and place wherein we have to make a painfully heartbreaking decision. A decision that in the end, is solely for the best.

There is a love that won't let go.
There is a hope that can't be broken.
There is an answer in the wind,
Going home to a prayer once spoken.

I hear the wind carrying the voices of a thousand prayers my way, drifting through the night, weaving through the leaves, talking in languages I never heard before, coming from souls I may never meet. There are words spoken long ago, finally landing in the places they are meant to be. There are whispers soaked with a mother's tears, circling the earth like a blanketing cloud. And the songs streaming through the silent air are from the fathers of days gone by. I hear the wind carrying ten thousand prayers your way, slipping past the veil, breaking through the vault, soaring across the sky, reaching lands you may never see. Open your door, look up to the stars, and listen to your ancestors speak.

I carry the heartache of many sorrows. I have waited patiently on forgiveness and held out for the faintest touch of understanding. I have stood over the broken pieces of a wrong decision. We are not unalike, you and I, and I have been lonely in life, too. I don't have a swift cure for loneliness, but if I could give you a soothing salve that could ease the discomfort of those desolate hours, believe me I would. For now, I will tell you—even your dark and isolating nights are hallowed ground. Even the air around you is scented with the fragrance of mercy. Even the center of your being is filled with consoling memories of those who love you. Even the thick breadth of night can't swallow you, instead holds you like a caring mother. For now, I will tell you. You may be all on your own, but you are never, ever alone in the silent struggle.

SONGBIRD

The heart knows.
Everything else is catching up.
So be patient with the struggle,
meld with the tide.

The truth isn't going anywhere
and no matter how strenuous,
change will draw us closer to it
according to our readiness,
based on our willingness.

When the songbird
sings into each morning,
all that's held inside
from its quiescent rest
wakes up
in time.

DON'T SHAME YOURSELF

Don't ever shame yourself for showing up, admitting or sharing, only to be shutdown or even ghosted. To want to reach out and describe your struggle and be understood is better than holding it all painfully inside and to never be seen. It's all humanly real. The risk to be honest and open. The exposure from connecting outside vulnerability. The enormous courage it takes to let your truth be revealed. And know in turn, not everyone can respond in the way you expect and believe—or perhaps at all, sometimes.

But, don't ever shame yourself.

Don't diminish your light for expressing or become conditioned to not ask for help in your time of great need.

EMPOWERMENT'S FIRST STEP

The moment a victim speaks publicly after holding in a traumatic truth over time, they risk entering an arena of societal judgement and questioning.

Why have you been silent?
How did this situation serve you?
What kind of person are you?

If you have somehow been managing to exist under the yoke of intimidation brought on by someone's attacking words, threats or abusive behavior, and one day step out into the light of admission, you are being a responsible person who can no longer hold the weight of another's wrongdoing so maliciously forced upon you.

You were violated when you were vulnerable. You then had to negotiate the subsequent internal aftermath and carry on privately, having little outside support with a great deal of uncertainty and fear bottled up inside. *You had to survive.*

Empowerment's first step is to listen to your own voice and allow your truth its rightful expression.

THE SILENT THINGS

I'm hungry these days
for the silent things.
The mystery in numbers.
The waking of slumber.
A single falling feather,

and the language of trees.

I'm craving in life
for what the
soundless bring.

The breath before dawn.
The blue within half-light.
The ascent of a sunrise,

and the thirst in your eyes.

Like poetry unheard of,
meaning builds up slowly.
pouring into my soul,
I swim in waves of utter passion
when I hear the reckless boldness,
all the euphonious whispers,
of each want and desire

of the silent things.

WHEN SHE FINALLY BELIEVES

When someone finally believes, the clouds part
and light pillars touch the earth in validation.

When someone finally believes, a thunder claps
and breaks into lightning to mark the moment.

When she finally believes in her voice,
she ends questioning herself.

She stops doubting her worth and values her story.
She's done punishing herself for bringing the truth,

and the heavens open inside her soul, and she knows
in her bones she was right all along for trusting her power.

THE BEAUTY OF SMALL

Let me paint for you the beauty of *small*…
Small words. Small observations.
Small greetings, short calls.

These are the bravest steps for someone shy,
someone hurt, someone trying to connect,
and someone healing from trauma.
Small steps. Coming out of hiding and
finally feeling safe enough to make the first move.
Small steps. relaxed and ready to practice healthy ways
to bridge and bond for the very first time.
Small steps, like a beautiful sunrise—
glimmering at first, before shining boldly.

THE PRACTICE OF SELF-FORGIVENESS

What I want, above all else, is for you to continually forgive yourself, just as I forgive myself. Make self-forgiveness your primary practice until you have formed a new way of caring for you. Understand you are not meant to carry the bleak weight of guilt or remorse, or be for the remainder of your days imprisoned by sorrow. Compassionately exercise this sacred clearing until your steps become guided by the clarity of your emerging truth.

Forgive yourself for the breakup, for losing your place, for allowing yourself to be in a position of exposure. For getting involved in the beginning of something new, or for being trapped inside not knowing how to respond, what to believe, who to trust, or what to do.

Forgive yourself for failing to get a grip. For inflicting self-harm. For stumbling as your balance was being jeopardized—and for finally falling down. Forgive yourself for the drama, the provocation, for turning on yourself, for repeating the same act and reacting to the same trigger. For the pressure. The ruins. The feeling of powerlessness. Feeling like you gave too much of yourself away, loved too much, opened too wide, let yourself be seen—all too soon and for the wrong reasons. Forgive yourself for all of these.

Forgive yourself for not knowing why. For not responding in the manner it was expected. For going numb, or for not being able to speak. For finally expressing something after the fact, not knowing what questions to ask, or for not knowing exactly what to say. Forgive yourself and release the shame.

Forgive yourself for giving in to a substance, for reaching for a crutch, for believing in a lie. For feeling like a child– and for crying in the night. Forgive your soul for trying to make it through an ungraceful moment. Forgive your body for collapsing from the weight of too heavy a burden. Forgive your heart for yielding before it was ready. Forgive yourself, at last, for saying you were too weak.

Forgive yourself for panicking, for not trusting in the unknown, for feeling like you let yourself be used and mislead. For not being understood, but slandered. For not being embraced, but mishandled. For the feelings of guilt and indignity brought on by any of these, forgive yourself and cease the incessant act of self-blame.

LOOK TO THE CLEARING

We walk through the same places in life,
we arrive at different times. We must gather the crop
from difficult and unpleasant seasons past
that will take us onward into new and lively fields.
Even after all these years, we are still learning—
as we water the ground with the tears of our woundedness,
and collect wisdom from the pain of blistering thorns.
And although we will not always understand
or ever really want to go where these awkward
and arduous seasons take us,
love explains,
all this will bring you closer to truth.
Love says,
you have folded yourself tight,
but when you are ready,
you will open again.

As you remind yourself
to breathe fresh forgiveness
into the hurt that has maimed you,
and as you walk away from the briar
that has scathed you,

look to the clearing
for love's guidance—
leading you unwaveringly,
each day,
to be renewed.

ABOUT THE AUTHOR

Susan Frybort is an American-born poet with a deep fascination for life and the human experience. Writing since she was a child, her poems and affirmations are a tapestry of wisdom and compassion that soften the heart's edges, calling us home. Previously published in *Elephant Journal*, *Vivid Life*, *Urban Howl*, and *Women for One*, she has published two inspiring books. Her first, the poetry collection *Hope is a Traveler*, was published in 2015 to rave reviews. 'Hope' engages the senses through imagery and metaphor. Her second book, *Open Passages*, is a special collection of meditations and affirmations that offer soothing balm to the weary soul. Susan enjoys traveling, creating art, and spending time in nature. She is a proud mother to her brilliant daughter, Lindsay. Susan currently lives in Canada with her husband, author Jeff Brown, and their beloved cat Lacy. You can connect with her work at www.susanfrybort.com.